The Angels' Little Instruction Book

The Angels' Little Instruction Book

LEARNING FROM GOD'S HEAVENLY MESSENGERS

BY EILEEN ELIAS FREEMAN

WARNER BOOKS

A Time Warner Company

Warner Books, Inc., 1271 Avenue of the Americas, New York, NY 10020

 A Time Warner Company

Printed in the United States of America
First Printing: November 1994
10 9 8 7 6 5 4 3 2 1

Library of Congress Cataloging-in-Publication Data
Freeman, Eileen E.
    The angels' little instruction book : learning from God's heavenly
messengers/Eileen Elias Freeman.
        p.   cm.
    ISBN 0-446-67121-5
    1. Angels—Quotations, maxims, etc. 2. Bible—Quotations.
I. Title.
BT966.2.F7 1994
235' .3—dc20   94-27922
                                                CIP

All quotations from the scriptures have been taken from the New Revised Standard Version,
copyright 1989 by the Division of Christian Education of the National Council of the
Churches of Christ in the United States of America and used by permission.

Book design by H Roberts Design

Cover design by Julia Kushnirsky

Introduction

*J*esus reminded us that the Kingdom of heaven is all around us—in our very midst, in fact—so is it any wonder that we are surrounded by angels, God's unseen messengers? These wise and loving creatures have been a part of our lives since the earth was created, and are known to Judaism, Christianity, Islam, and other world religions. The scriptures tell us that angels are immortal spirits created by God as servants of the divine and guardians of the earth and all who dwell on it.

I have always believed in angels. When I was a child of five, God sent my angel into my life to comfort me after the death of my grandmother, and to reassure me that she was with God and that I need not fear anything in life. I have always tried to live that message.

That visitation awakened in me a hunger to find out more about the loving God who took pity on my grief and sent me such exquisite comfort. I wanted to learn all I could about the messengers and servants of God. I earned a B.A. in Comparative Religions from Barnard College, and an M.A. in Theology from the University of Notre Dame while pursuing my quest.

I now head The AngelWatch Foundation, Inc., a non-profit organization whose purpose is to search out evidence of angelic activity on earth and to disseminate information about angels. I publish *AngelWatch*, a bi-monthly magazine about angels that includes first-person accounts of angelic visitations, reviews of new books, and both scholarly and popular articles on angels. For more information about the work of The AngelWatch Foundation, please write to me at: AngelWatch, P.O. Box 1397, Mountainside, New Jersey 07092 U.S.A., enclosing a stamped, self-addressed envelope.

A word about the scripture texts used in this book: The quotes below each angelic "instruction" are not "proof texts" in the usual sense of the word. Rather, they are designed to provide a context within which we can see how God's angels operate on earth. Sometimes neither the "instruction" nor the relevant scripture mentions angels at all. Nonetheless, issues like forgiveness, love of neighbor, turning from evil, and living in the light of God are all matters of intense interest to our guardian angels.

In the end, we must realize that the angels have no instructions of their own to offer us. Like pure prisms, they simply refract for us a small portion of the infinitely faceted crystal that is God. Whatever comes from an angel came first from God, who delights in providing us with wonders at every step of our journey Home. May we "run with perseverance the race that is set before us," holding hands with the angels and our brothers and sisters, and always looking to Jesus, "the pioneer and perfecter of our faith."

Eileen Elias Freeman

April, 1994

The Angels' Little Instruction Book

*We are never closer to our angels
than when we pray to God.*

☙

*I give you thanks, O Lord, with my whole heart;
before the angels I sing your praise.*
Psalm 138:1

Children often have imaginary playmates. I suspect that half of them are really their guardian angels.

❧

Take care that you do not despise one of these little ones; for I tell you, in heaven their angels continually see the face of my Father.
Matthew 18:10

Never be afraid.
Fear is the most useless gift
we can give ourselves.

Do not be afraid; for see, I am bringing you good news of great joy
for all the people: To you is born this day in the city of
David a Savior, who is the Messiah, the Lord.
Luke 2:10-11

Angels shine from without because their spirits are lit from within by the light of God.

An angel of the Lord, descending from heaven, came and rolled back the stone and sat on it. His appearance was like lightning and his clothing white as snow.
Matthew 28:3

Angels can fly lightly
because they take God seriously.

❧

While I was praying, . . . Gabriel, whom I had seen before
in a vision came to me in swift flight at the
time of the evening sacrifice.
Daniel 9:21

*Our angels know us
more intimately than our parents,
our spouses, or ourselves.*

❧

My lord has wisdom like the wisdom of the angel of
God to know all things that are on the earth.
2 Samuel 14:20

Angels speak to us with the voice of the God who sent them.

❧

I am going to send an angel in front of you,
to guard you on the way. . .
Be attentive to him and listen to his voice. . .
for my name is in him.
Exodus 23:20-21

Life is a tapestry:
We are the warp; angels, the weft;
God, the Weaver: Only the Weaver
sees the whole design.

My frame was not hidden from you when I was being made in secret,
intricately woven in the depths of the earth.
Psalm 139:15

An angel falls from heaven
with each drop of rain,
to guide it to its place.

≈

Who has cut a channel for the torrents of rain
and a way for the thunderbolt?
Job 38:25

Insight is better than eyesight when it comes to seeing an angel.

❧

I, Daniel, alone saw the vision; the people who were with me did not
see the vision, though a great trembling fell upon them,
and they fled and hid themselves.
So I was left alone to see this great vision.
Daniel 10:7-8

If we could speak with the tongues of angels, our first word would always be <u>God</u>.

And one (seraph) called to another and said:
"Holy, holy, holy is the Lord of hosts."
Isaiah 6:3

Keep your heart open,
like the angels';
a closed heart can neither give
nor receive love.

≈

A new heart I will give you, and a new spirit I will put within you;
and I will remove from your body the heart of stone
and give you a heart of flesh.
Ezekiel 36:26

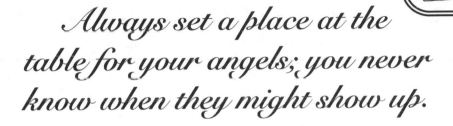

Always set a place at the table for your angels; you never know when they might show up.

Abraham said, "My lord, If I have found favor with you, do not pass by your servant. . . . let me bring a little bread, that you may refresh yourselves." Genesis 18:3, 5

Angels have no need
of wings — they soar aloft
on the strong currents of love.

~

If I take the wings of the morning and settle at
the farthest limits of the sea, even there your hand shall lead me,
and your right hand shall hold me fast.
Psalm 139:9-10

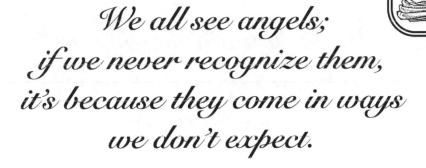

We all see angels;
if we never recognize them,
it's because they come in ways
we don't expect.

Do not neglect to show hospitality to strangers,
for by doing that some have entertained angels
without knowing it.
Hebrews 13:2

When babies look beyond you and giggle, maybe they're seeing angels.

Jesus said, "I thank you, Father, Lord of heaven and earth, because you have hidden these things from the wise and intelligent and have revealed them to infants."
Matthew 11:25

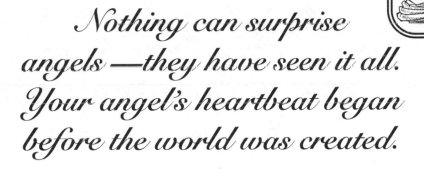

Nothing can surprise angels —they have seen it all. Your angel's heartbeat began before the world was created.

The Lord created me at the beginning of his work,
the first of his acts of long ago. Ages ago I was set up, at the first,
before the beginning of the earth.
Proverbs 8:22-23

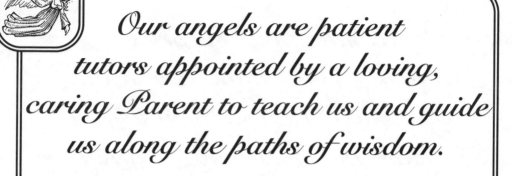

Our angels are patient tutors appointed by a loving, caring Parent to teach us and guide us along the paths of wisdom.

When I, Daniel, had seen the vision, I tried to understand it.
Then someone appeared standing before me, having the appearance of a man,
and I heard a human voice by the Ulai calling, "Gabriel,
help this man understand the vision."
Daniel 8:15-16

Angels are not freelance operators; like Jesus, they come to do the will of the One who sends them.

Bless the Lord, O you his angels, you mighty ones who
do his bidding, obedient to his spoken word. Bless the Lord,
all his hosts, his ministers who do his will.
Psalm 103:20-21

*An angel's love and devotion
are unconditional, because God's
faithfulness knows no limits.*

~

Appoint steadfast love and faithfulness to watch over him.
So I will always sing praises to your name. . .
Psalm 61:7b-8a

Talk with your angel as you would talk to any of your close friends — honestly and often.

Some friends play at friendship, but a true friend
sticks closer than one's nearest kin.
Proverbs 18:24

Even Jesus had a guardian angel.

~

For it is clear that (Jesus) did not come to help angels,
but the descendants of Abraham. Therefore he had to become like
his brothers and sisters in every respect, so that he might be
a merciful and faithful high priest in the service of God.
Hebrews 2:16-17

*Being sorry feeds the ego;
being forgiven feeds the spirit.*

～

*For godly grief produces a repentance that leads to salvation
and brings no regret, but worldly grief produces death.*
2 Corinthians 7:10

A pacifist is different from a passivist —one lives in peace, the other, in pieces.

Seek peace and pursue it.
Psalm 34:14

*Let us love the world
to peace.*

❧

Pray for the peace of Jerusalem.
Psalm 122:6

The more you live in the Light of God, the less power the darkness has over your life.

≈

*If we walk in the light, as He himself is in the light,
we have fellowship with one another, and the blood of Jesus
his Son cleanses us from all sin.*
1 John 1:7

We need to forgive and be forgiven if we would heal our lives.

☙

"But so you may know that the Son of Man has the authority to forgive sins"—(Jesus) said to the one who was paralyzed—
"I say to you, stand up and take your bed and go to your home."
Luke 5:24

*Forgiveness begins in the will;
healing our feelings comes later.*

❦

*Then Jesus said, "Father, forgive them,
for they do not know what they are doing."*
Luke 23:34

It isn't the size of the gift that matters, but the size of the heart that gives it.

Blessed are the pure in heart, for they will see God.
Matthew 5:8

Keep your good deeds for others a secret, just as your angel works behind the scenes in your own life.

≈

But when you give alms, do not let your left hand know what
your right hand is doing, so that your alms may be done in secret;
and your Father who sees in secret will reward you.
Matthew 6:3-4

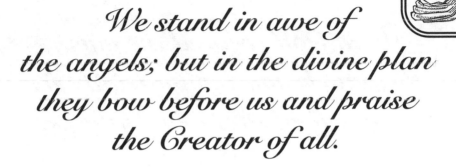

We stand in awe of the angels; but in the divine plan they bow before us and praise the Creator of all.

What are human beings that you are mindful of them, mortals, that you care for them? Yet you have made them little lower than the angels, and crowned them with glory and honor.
Psalm 8:4-5

*When God created the earth,
the angels sang with delight as
they helped shape its features.*

❧

When he marked out the foundations of the earth, then I was beside him,
like a master worker; rejoicing before him always, rejoicing in
his inhabited world and delighting in the human race.
Proverbs 8:29b-31

*When we freely forgive
others who have hurt us,
our angel brings us a special
blessing of love from God.*

I tell you, there is joy in the presence of the angels
of God over one sinner who repents.
Luke 15:10

Our angels cradle our every prayer in their hands, laying it confidently before the throne of God.

❧

For even now my witness is in heaven, and he that vouches for me
is on high, the interpreter of my thoughts to God.
Job 16:19-20

For every angel whose ministry is on earth, a million angels praise God in heaven.

❧

A thousand thousands served him, and ten thousand times
ten thousand stood attending him.
Daniel 7:10

*Whether we are filled
with joy or grief, our angels
are close to us, speaking to
our hearts of God's love.*

❧

The angel of the Lord encamps around those
who fear him and delivers them.
Psalm 34:7

Angels are principally the guardians of our spirits. Their function is not to do our work for us, but to help us do it ourselves, by God's grace.

(Jesus prayed) "Father, if you are willing, remove this cup from me; yet not my will but yours be done." Then an angel from heaven appeared to him and gave him strength.
Luke 22:42-43

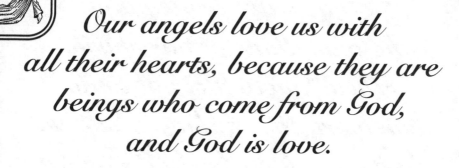

*Our angels love us with
all their hearts, because they are
beings who come from God,
and God is love.*

❧

Beloved, let us love one another, because love is from God;
everyone who loves is born of God and knows God.
Whoever does not love, does not know God, for God is love.
1 John 4:7-8

*Angels watch over
every cell in our bodies,
every beat of our hearts.
They take note of
everything we do.*

Therefore, since we are surrounded by so great a cloud of witnesses,
let us also lay aside every weight and that sin the clings so closely.
Hebrews 12:1

*We can trust that every
word an angel speaks
to our heart is right
and suitable to our needs.*

❧

*Your servant thought, "The word of my lord the king
will set me at rest"; for my lord the king is like
the angel of God, discerning good and evil.*
2 Samuel 14:17

*If you can't save the
whole world, at least save
your own backyard.*

❧

You have been trustworthy in a few things;
I will put you in charge of many things.
Matthew 25:21

When we follow the
inspirations of our angels,
they direct our steps toward God.

❧

Teach me to do your will, for you are my God.
Let your good spirit lead me on a level path.
Psalm 143:10

*Guardian angels never
take vacations.*

*He will not let your foot be moved; he who keeps you
will not slumber. He who keeps Israel will
neither slumber nor sleep.*
Psalm 121:3-4

*An angel's words to us
are full of power and love
because they come from
the Word Himself.*

Set a guard over my mouth, O Lord;
keep watch over the door of my lips.
Psalm 141:3

Everyone who has ever lived on the face of the earth has had a guardian angel.

❧

He makes his sun rise on the evil and on the good,
and sends rain on the righteous
and on the unrighteous.
Matthew 5:45

The name Michael
in Hebrew asks the question,
"Who is like God?"
and answers it: No one.

❧

Thus says. . . the Lord of hosts: I am the first and I am the last;
besides me there is no god. Who is like me?
Let them proclaim it. . . Is there any god besides me?. . .
I know not one.
Isaiah 44:6-7a, 8b

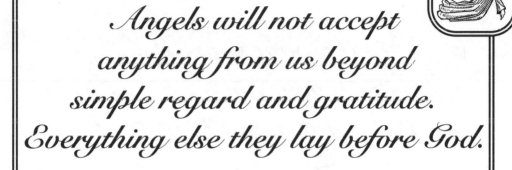

*Angels will not accept
anything from us beyond
simple regard and gratitude.
Everything else they lay before God.*

❧

*The angel of the Lord said to Manoah, "If you detain me,
I will not eat your food, but if you want to prepare a burnt offering,
then offer it to the Lord."*
Judges 13:16

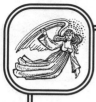

*The only source of
nourishment for an angel is
the joyful worship of God.*

My food is to do the will of him who sent me
and to complete his work.
John 4:34

Our angels are closer to us than ever when we are sad or in trouble.

❧

"Comfort, O comfort my people," says your God.
"Speak tenderly to the heart of Jerusalem. . ."
Isaiah 40:1-2a

*Your guardian angel is
a friend for life —
eternal life.*

❧

*Say to wisdom, "You are my sister,"
and call insight your intimate friend.*
Proverbs 7:4

*Angels teach us lessons
that we cannot learn in
any other school.*

❧

*The spirit of the Lord shall rest upon him, the spirit of
wisdom and understanding, the spirit of counsel and might,
the spirit of knowledge and the fear of the Lord.*
Isaiah 11:2

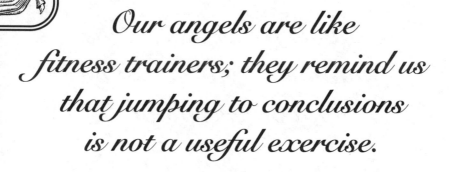

*Our angels are like
fitness trainers; they remind us
that jumping to conclusions
is not a useful exercise.*

❧

Do not judge by appearances,
but judge by right judgment.
John 7:24

Our guardian angels begin their loving care when we are conceived, not when we are born.

When Elizabeth heard Mary's greeting, the child leaped in her womb.
And Elizabeth was filled with the Holy Spirit and exclaimed
with a loud cry, "Blessed are you among women, and
blessed is the fruit of your womb."
Luke 1:41-42

Be an angel to someone else whenever you can, as a way of thanking God for the help your angel has given you.

Do not neglect to do good and to share what you have,
for such sacrifices are pleasing to God.
Hebrews 13:16

*Guardian angels are
consistent, insistent,
and persistent.*

❧

*Elijah lay down under the broom tree and fell asleep.
Suddenly an angel touched him and said, "Get up and eat."... He ate and
drank and lay down again. The angel of the Lord came
a second time and said, "Get up and eat, otherwise the journey
will be too much for you." He got up and ate and drank;
then he went in the strength of that food forty days and forty nights.*
1 Kings 19:4-7

Angels can make mistakes, too.

❧

Even in his servants he puts no trust, and
his angels he charges with error; how much more those
who live in houses of clay, whose foundation is the dust,
who are crushed like a moth.
Job 4:18-19

*We should thank God
with great joy and happiness for
sending His angels into our lives.*

❧

*As for the holy ones in the land, they are the noble,
in whom is all my delight*
Psalm 16:3

The angels' first and most important task is the perfect worship of God, who created them.

※

And Ezra said, "You are the Lord, you alone; you have made heaven, the heaven of heavens, with all their host, the earth and all that is on it, the seas and all that is in them. To all of them you give life, and the host of heaven worships you."
Nehemiah 9:6

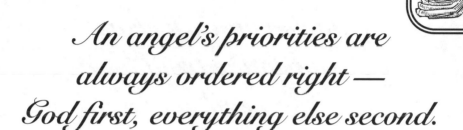

*An angel's priorities are
always ordered right —
God first, everything else second.*

❦

Ascribe to the Lord, O heavenly beings, ascribe to
the Lord glory and strength. Ascribe to the Lord the glory
of his name; worship the Lord in holy splendor.
Psalm 29:1-2

*Angels can deliver us,
even when the troubles in
our lives really heat up.*

≈

Then King Nebuchadnezzar said . . .
"Was it not three men that we threw bound into the fire? . . .
But I see four men, unbound, and the fourth has
the appearance of a son of the gods."
Daniel 3:24-25

*The angels are such
an ancient race that we are
as children by comparison.*

❧

*Where were you when I laid the foundation of the earth? . . .
On what were its bases sunk, or who laid its cornerstone when
the morning stars sang together and all the
sons of God shouted for joy?*
Job 38:4a, 6-7

Angels don't leave messages on our answering machines. We must pick up the phone ourselves.

❧

Then the angel of God said to me in the dream, "Jacob," and I said, "Here I am!"
Genesis 31:11

An angel's "real" name
is known only to God and
the other angels — so give your
angel any name you choose.

≈

Then Manoah said to the angel of the Lord,
"What is your name, so that we may honor you
when your words come true?" But the angel of the Lord
said to him, "Why do you ask my name? It is too wonderful."
Judges 13:17-18

*An angel is a sign of
God's constant care
and compassion.*

❧

Our ancestors went down to Egypt, and we lived in Egypt a long time;
and the Egyptians oppressed us and our ancestors,
and when we cried to the Lord, he heard our voice
and sent an angel and brought us out of Egypt.
Numbers 20:15-16

You can't fool
an angel.

The (angel of the) Lord said to Abraham,
"Why did Sarah laugh and say, 'Shall I indeed bear a child,
now that I am old?' Is anything too wonderful for the Lord? . . ."
But Sarah denied, saying, "I did not laugh";
for she was afraid. He said, "Oh yes, you did laugh."
Genesis 18:13-14a, 15

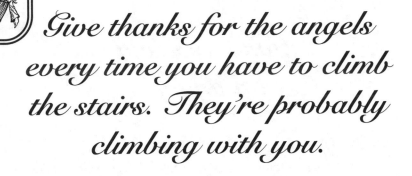

Give thanks for the angels every time you have to climb the stairs. They're probably climbing with you.

And (Jacob) dreamed that there was a stairway set up on the earth,
the top of it reaching to heaven, and the angels
of God were ascending and descending on it.
Genesis 28:12

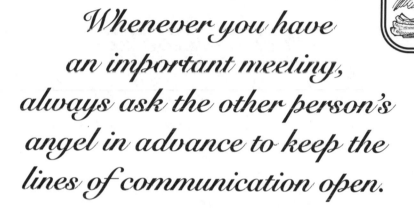

*Whenever you have
an important meeting,
always ask the other person's
angel in advance to keep the
lines of communication open.*

❦

The Lord, before whom I walk, will send his angel with you
and make your way successful.
Genesis 24:40

Angels can look just like us, or they can appear like nothing on earth.

❧

Each had four faces, and each of them had four wings.
Their legs were straight, and the soles of their feet were like the sole of
a calf's foot; and they sparkled like burnished bronze.
Under their wings on their four sides they had human hands.
Ezekiel 1:6-9a

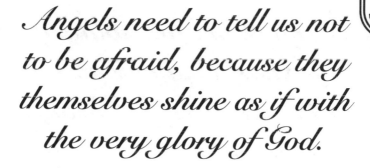

Angels need to tell us not to be afraid, because they themselves shine as if with the very glory of God.

≈

Then the woman came and told her husband,
"A man of God came to me, and his appearance was
like that of an angel, most awe-inspiring."
Judges 13:6

Angels are not solitary hermits; they belong to a loving society of beings united by the love of God.

So then you are no longer strangers and aliens, but you are citizens
with the saints and also members of the household of God.
Ephesians 2:19

Even the rulers of this world have been given into the hands of heavenly princes.

When the Most High apportioned the nations, when he divided humankind, he fixed the boundaries of the peoples according to the number of the gods; the Lord's own portion was his people, Jacob his allotted share.
Deuteronomy 32:8-9

How many angels are there? God only knows!

Then I looked, and I heard the voice of many angels
surrounding the throne and the living creatures and the elders;
they numbered myriads of myriads and thousands of thousands.
Revelation 5:11

When life gets rocky,
God's angels smooth the path
for our hearts so we can
reach out for help.

❧

For he will command his angels concerning you to guard you
in all your ways. On their hands they will bear you up,
so that you will not dash your foot against a stone.
Psalm 91:11-12

When we worship God,
our angels add their prayers
and turn our single voices
into hundred-part harmony.

☙

Then I heard every creature in heaven and on earth and under
the earth and in the sea, and all that is in them, singing,
"To the One seated on the throne and to the Lamb,
be blessing and honor and glory and might forever and ever!"
Revelation 5:13

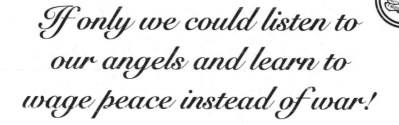

If only we could listen to our angels and learn to wage peace instead of war!

How beautiful upon the mountains are the feet of
the messenger who announces peace, who brings good news,
who announces salvation, who says to Zion,
"Your God reigns."
Isaiah 52:7

If angels rarely appear,
it's because we all too often
mistake the medium
for the Message.

❧

Then I fell down at (the angel's) feet to worship him, but he said to me,
"You must not do that! I am a fellow servant with you and
your comrades who hold the testimony of Jesus. Worship God!"
Revelation 19:10

*If we want to approach
God, we must let His angels'
fire purify our hearts and burn
away our self-centeredness.*

❧

*The seraph touched my mouth with (the burning coal) and said,
"Now that this has touched your lips, your guilt has
departed and your sin is blotted out."*
Isaiah 6:7

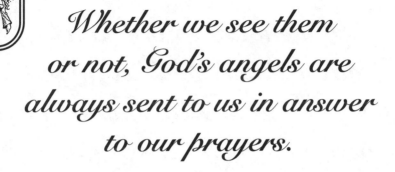

Whether we see them or not, God's angels are always sent to us in answer to our prayers.

(Gabriel) said to me, "Do not fear, Daniel, for from the first day that you set your mind to gain understanding and to humble yourself before your God, your words have been heard, and I have come because of your words."
Daniel 10:12

We give the fallen angels far too much free publicity. For myself, I choose to look only to Jesus, and to the angels who do His will.

❧

Let us run with perseverance the race that is set before us, looking to Jesus the pioneer and perfecter of our faith, who for the joy that was set before him endured the cross, disregarding its shame, and has taken his seat at the right hand of the throne of God.
Hebrews 12:1b-2

Listen! Do you hear all around you the sounds of God's angels doing battle for the Kingdom?

❧

And war broke out in heaven; Michael and his angels fought
against the dragon. The dragon and his angels fought back,
but they were defeated.
Revelation 12:7-8

Gabriel means "Strong One of God"; and we are all Gabriels when we lean on the Lord for strength.

≈

Again one in human form touched me and strengthened me.
He said, "Do not fear, greatly beloved, you are safe.
Be strong and courageous." When he spoke to me,
I was strengthened and said, "Let my lord speak,
for you have strengthened me."
Daniel 10:18-19

*If we want to fly with
the angels, we must first walk
the path of humility.*

Whoever becomes humble like this child is the greatest
in the kingdom of heaven.
Matthew 18:4

If an angel gives you a message, act on it at once.

When Joseph awoke from sleep, he did as the angel
of the Lord commanded him.
Matthew 1:24

*Pay attention to
your dreams —
God's angels often speak
directly to our hearts
when we are asleep.*

❧

I slept, but my heart was awake. Listen!
my beloved is knocking. "Open to me, my sister, my love,
my dove, my perfect one . . ."
Song of Solomon 5:2

*The brightness of
the angels reflects the clarity
they bring into our lives.*

❧

Then I said (to the angel), "What are these, my lord?"
The angel who talked with me said to me,
"I will show you what they are."
Zechariah 1:9

Don't let the cute cherubs of Victorian art fool you —the angels of God are anything but wimps.

❦

"See, I am sending my messenger to prepare the way before me . . .
The messenger of the covenant in whom you delight,
indeed he is coming," says the Lord of hosts.
"But who can endure the day of his coming and who can stand
when he appears? For he is like a refiner's fire . . ."
Malachi 3:1-2

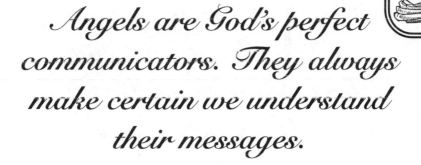

Angels are God's perfect communicators. They always make certain we understand their messages.

(Gabriel) said to me, "Daniel, greatly beloved,
pay attention to the word that I am going to speak to you.
Stand on your feet, for I have now been sent to you."
Daniel 10:11

*When we ask our angels
to pray for us, we can
be sure we have friends
in the highest places.*

❧

*Then if there should be for one of them an angel, a mediator,
one of a thousand, one who declares a person upright, and
he is gracious to that person and says, "Deliver him from
going down into the Pit; I have found a ransom . . ."*
Job 23:33-34

Beneath their tranquil surface, angels are creatures of deep emotion and feeling.

Then the angel of the Lord said, "O Lord of hosts,
how long will you withhold mercy from Jerusalem and the cities
of Judah, with which you have been angry these seventy years?"
Then the Lord replied with gracious and comforting words to
the angel who talked with me.
Zechariah 1:12-13

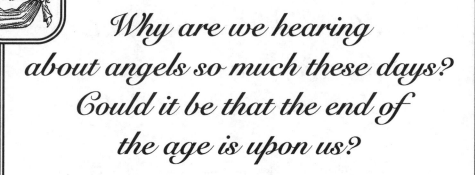

Why are we hearing about angels so much these days? Could it be that the end of the age is upon us?

❧

Then he will send out the angels, and gather his elect
from the four winds, from the ends of the earth
to the ends of heaven.
Mark 13:27

*Angels have no agenda
of their own.
Every message they bring to us
comes from God.*

❧

*Jesus said to him, "Away with you, Satan! for it is written,
'Worship the Lord your God and serve only him.'"
Then the devil left him and suddenly angels
came and waited on him.*
Matthew 4:10-11

Angels are direct creations
of God, each one a
unique Master's piece.

For in the resurrection they neither marry nor are given in marriage,
but are like the angels in heaven.
Matthew 22:30

Jesus alone is Lord of the angels.

❧

At the name of Jesus, every knee should bend,
in heaven and on earth and under the earth,
and every tongue should confess that Jesus Christ is Lord,
to the glory of God the Father.
Philippians 2:10-11

Even the angels —
as full of wisdom as they are —
don't know everything.

But about that day and hour no one knows,
neither the angels of heaven, nor the Son,
but only the Father.
Matthew 24:36

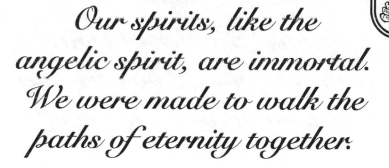

Our spirits, like the angelic spirit, are immortal. We were made to walk the paths of eternity together.

Jesus said to them: ". . . Indeed they cannot die anymore, because they are like angels and are children of God, being children of the resurrection."
Luke 20:36

Raphael, whose name means "Healer of God," is the angel God has set over the healing of all the earth.

❧

(In the five porticoes of the pool of Bethesda) lay many invalids . . . waiting for the stirring of the water; for an angel of the Lord went down at certain seasons into the pool and stirred up the water; whoever stepped in first after the stirring of the water was made well from whatever disease that person had.

John 5:3-4

Put your trust firmly in God — but lock your house up when you leave.

Then the devil took him to Jerusalem and placed him on the pinnacle
of the temple, saying, "If you are the Son of God,
throw yourself down from here, for it is written,
'He will command his angels concerning you to protect you . . .'"
Jesus answered him, "It is said, 'Do not put the Lord
your God to the test.'"
Luke 4:9-10, 12

*The message of a true
angel of God is like an apple:
always sweet, refreshing,
and nourishing.*

✍

No good tree bears bad fruit, nor again does a bad tree bear good fruit;
for each tree is known by its own fruit. Figs are not gathered from thorns,
nor are grapes picked from a bramble bush.
Luke 6:43-45

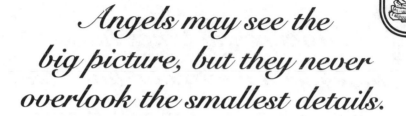

Angels may see the big picture, but they never overlook the smallest details.

(The angel) tapped Peter on the side, and woke him, saying,
"Get up quickly." And the chains fell off his wrists.
The angel said to him, "Fasten your belt and put on your sandals."
He did so. Then he said to him,
"Wrap your cloak around you and follow me."
Acts 12:7-8

How many times have angels come into our lives and we never recognized them?

~

Peter went out and followed (the angel); he did not realize
that what was happening with the angel's help was real;
he thought he was seeing a vision.
Acts 12:9

Angels have extraordinary God-given powers over the natural world that we can only guess at.

❧

(Peter and the angel) came before the iron gate leading into the city. It opened for them of its own accord . . .
Acts 12:10

*God's care for us
is measured in immensities,
not minimums.*

❧

Do you think that I cannot appeal to my Father,
and he will at once send me more than
twelve legions of angels?
Matthew 26:53

*Angels are all around us,
all the time, in the
very air we breathe.*

❧

The kingdom of God is not coming with things that can be observed;
nor will they say to you, "Look, here it is!" or
"There it is!" For, in fact, the kingdom
of God is among you.
Luke 17:20-21

Unfortunately, not everything that claims to be an angel of God really is. We must learn to tell the difference.

～

Even Satan disguises himself as an angel of light.
So it is not strange that his ministers also disguise themselves
as ministers of righteousness.
2 Corinthians 11:14-15

Just suppose the person ahead of you in the supermarket this morning was really *an angel* . . .

❦

You know that it was because of a physical infirmity that I first announced the gospel to you; though my condition put you to the test, you did not scorn or despise me, but welcomed me as an angel of God, as Christ Jesus.
Galatians 4:13-14

Ask the guardian angel of your church for help in building the body of Christ in your town.

To the angel of the church in Ephesus write: These are the words
of him who holds the seven stars in his right hand,
who walks among the seven golden lampstands.
Revelation 2:1

If we could burn with the
ardent love of the seraphim,
we could heal our lives
in an instant.

Moses . . . came to Horeb, the mountain of God.
There the angel of the Lord appeared to him in a flame of fire
out of a bush; he looked, and the bush was blazing,
yet it was not consumed.
Exodus 3:1-2

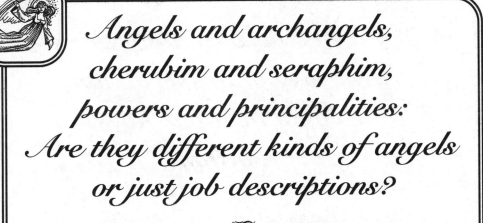

Angels and archangels,
cherubim and seraphim,
powers and principalities:
Are they different kinds of angels
or just job descriptions?

(Jesus) is the image of the invisible God, the firstborn of all creation;
for in him all things in heaven and on earth were created, things visible
and invisible, whether thrones or dominions or rulers or powers.
Colossians 1:15

If we could purify our hearts of all the darkness still within, oh, what wonders we would see all around us!

❧

You have come to Mount Zion, and to the city of the living God, . . . and to innumerable angels in festal gathering, and to the assembly of the firstborn who are enrolled in heaven, and to God . . .
Hebrews 12:22-23

*How wonderful it must be
to speak the language of
the angels, with no words for hate
and a million words for love!*

~

If I speak in the tongues of mortals and of angels,
but do not have love, I am a noisy gong or a clanging cymbal.
1 Corinthians 13:1

Even angels can agree to disagree in a good cause.

❧

Then (Gabriel) said, . . . "Now I must return to fight against the prince of Persia, and when I am through with him, the prince of Greece will come . . . There is no one with me who contends against these princes, except Michael, your prince."
Daniel 10:20, 21b

Angels were the first matchmakers.

≈

The Lord, before whom I walk, will send his angel with you and make your way successful. You shall get a wife for my son from my kindred, from my father's house.
Genesis 24:40.

Angels can fly because
they carry no burdens.

Take my yoke upon you and learn from me; for I am gentle
and humble in heart, and you will find rest for your souls.
For my yoke is easy, and my burden is light.
Matthew 11:29-30

*Listening to the angel
within brings special
help from God.*

≈

*If you listen to (the angel's) voice and do all that I say,
then I will be an enemy to your enemies
and a foe to your foes.*
Exodus 23:22

Angels are never rash;
they always exercise
good judgment.

❦

But my lord the king is like the angel of God;
do therefore what seems good to you.
2 Samuel 19:27

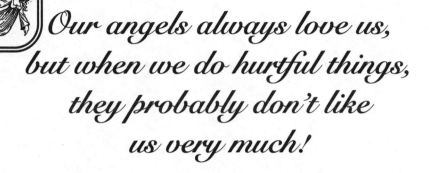

*Our angels always love us,
but when we do hurtful things,
they probably don't like
us very much!*

❧

The angel of the Lord said to (Balaam),
"Why have you struck your donkey these three times?
I have come out as an adversary,
because your way is perverse before me."
Numbers 22:32

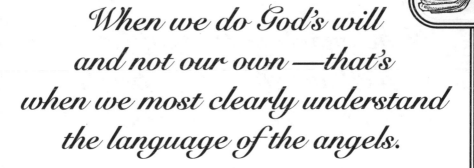

*When we do God's will
and not our own —that's
when we most clearly understand
the language of the angels.*

❧

*Your kingdom come. Your will be done on earth,
as it is in heaven.*
Matthew 6:10

The angels of God will never feed our egos; they prefer to nourish our spirits.

❧

Come, let us go down, and confuse their language there,
so that they will not understand one another's speech.
Genesis 11:7

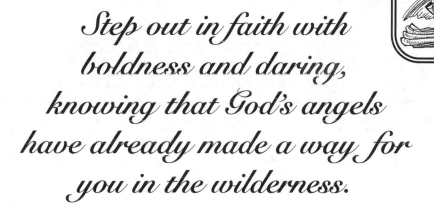

Step out in faith with boldness and daring, knowing that God's angels have already made a way for you in the wilderness.

Every valley shall be lifted up and every mountain shall be made low; the uneven ground shall become level, and the rough places a plain.
Isaiah 40:4

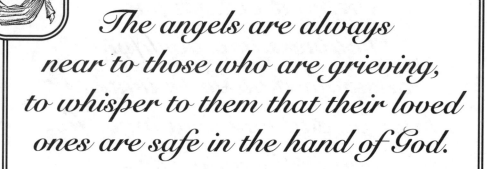

The angels are always near to those who are grieving, to whisper to them that their loved ones are safe in the hand of God.

Mary stood weeping outside the tomb. As she wept, she bent over
to look into the tomb; and she saw two angels in white. . . .
They said to her, "Woman, why are you weeping?"
John 20:11-13a

*When our mortal eyes
close on this world for
the last time, our angels open
our spiritual eyes and escort us
personally before the face of God.*

For I know that my redeemer lives, and that at the last he will
stand upon the earth; and after my skin has been thus destroyed,
then without my flesh I shall see God.
Job 19:25-26

The devil is not the opposite of God, but of Michael.

❧

When the archangel Michael contended with the devil and
disputed about the body of Moses, he did not dare to bring
a condemnation of slander against him, but said,
"The Lord rebuke you!"
Jude 9

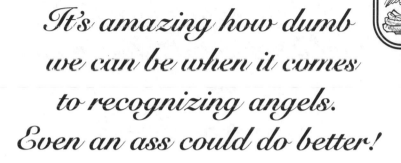

*It's amazing how dumb
we can be when it comes
to recognizing angels.
Even an ass could do better!*

❧

*Now (Balaam) was riding his donkey, and his two servants
were with him. The donkey saw the angel of the Lord
standing in the road, with a drawn sword in his hand;
so the donkey turned off the road and went into the field.*
Numbers 22:22-23

*I think sometimes that
God has placed hard things
in the scriptures just
to teach us humility.*

❧

*When people began to multiply on the face of the ground, and daughters
were born to them, the sons of God saw that they were fair; and they took
wives for themselves of all that they chose . . . The Nephilim were on
the earth in those days . . . when the sons of God went in to the daughters
of humans, who bore children to them. These were the heroes . . .*
Genesis 6:1-2, 4

If we have the mind of Christ, his light will shine not only in our hearts but in our faces as well.

And all who sat in the council looked intently at (Stephen),
and they saw that his face was like the face of an angel.
Acts 6:15

Nothing exceeds the exquisite courtesy of an angel.

❧

And (Gabriel) came to (Mary) and said,
"Greetings, favored one. The Lord is with you."
Luke 1:28

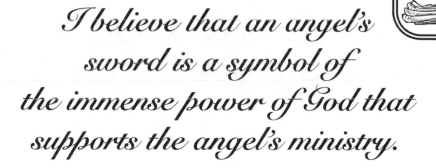

I believe that an angel's swoard is a symbol of the immense power of God that supports the angel's ministry.

David looked up and saw the angel of the Lord standing between earth and heaven, and in his hand a drawn sword stretched out over Jerusalem.
1 Chronicles 21:16

*Any spiritual being
we can summon at will
is not an angel of God.*

≈

*So Saul disguised himself . . . and came to the (medium at Endor)
by night. And he said, "Consult a spirit for me, and
bring up for me the one whom I name to you." . . .
Then the woman said, "Whom shall I bring up for you?"*
1 Samuel 28:8, 11

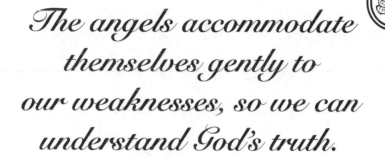

The angels accommodate themselves gently to our weaknesses, so we can understand God's truth.

❧

(The angel) also measured its wall, one hundred forty-four cubits
by human measurement, which the angel was using.
Revelation 21:17

*Angels are like clear glass —
only visible until
the Son shines through
the window of the soul.*

❧

He must increase, but I must decrease.
John 3:30

*Angels fly at light speed,
because they are servants
of the Light.*

❧

He rode on a cherub and flew; he came swiftly
upon the wings of the wind.
Psalm 18:10

Angels never compel;
instead, they invite.
Angels never interfere with
our free choice.

An angel of the Lord appeared to him in a dream and said,
"Joseph, son of David, do not be afraid to take Mary as your wife,
for the child conceived in her is from the Holy Spirit. . . ."
Matthew 1:20

Angels always make their messages clear, because they are the most perfect communicators in the universe.

❧

Zechariah said to the angel, "How will I know that this is so? For I am an old man, and my wife is getting on in years." The angel replied, "I am Gabriel. I stand in the presence of God, and I have been sent to speak to you and to bring you this good news."
Luke 1:18-19

When you suddenly feel a sense of confidence and trust in God, know that your guardian angel is very close to you.

❧

Then Mary said, "Here am I, the servant of the Lord;
let it be with me according to your word."
Luke 1:38

*God not only sends
special angels into our lives,
but sometimes He even sends
them back again if we forget to
take notes the first time!*

❧

Then Manoah entreated the Lord and said, "O Lord, I pray,
let the man of God whom you sent come to us again and teach us . . ."
God listened to Manoah, and the angel of God came again.
Judges 13:8

"Angel" means "messenger";
so, in a sense, we really can be
angels of God's truth to others.

~

Then Haggai, the messenger of the Lord, spoke to
the people with the Lord's message, saying,
"'I am with you,' says the Lord."
Haggai 1:13

As servants of God,
angels are part of
the household of Christ,
not the body of Christ.

❧

For to which of the angels did God ever say,
"You are my son; today I have begotten you"?
Or again, "I will be his father, and he will be my son"?
Hebrews 1:5

Angels need no faith or hope, because they already see God unveiled. For an angel, love and service are all.

❧

And now faith, hope, and love abide, these three;
and the greatest of these is love.
1 Corinthians 13:13

If your angel has helped you today, give the praise and glory to God.

❧

Nebuchadnezzar said, "Blessed be the God of Shadrach, Meshach, and Abednego, who has sent his angel and delivered his servants who trusted in him."
Daniel 3:28

Cleanliness —
of spirit —
is next to godliness.

❧

Now Joshua was dressed with filthy clothes as he stood before the angel.
The angel said to those who were standing before him,
"Take off his filthy clothes." And to him he said,
"See, I have taken your guilt away from you,
and I will clothe you with festal apparel."
Zechariah 3:3-4

Learn all you can about the angels, for they will lead you to God.

❧

The fear of the Lord is the beginning of wisdom, and knowledge of the holy ones is insight.
Proverbs 9:10

Share an angel's message —
sometimes it's not meant just
for our own hearts, but
for others' as well.

(The angel said) "Mortal, look closely and listen attentively, and
set your mind upon all that I shall show you, for you were brought
here in order that I might show you; declare all that
you see to the house of Israel."
Ezekiel 40:4

An angel of God is peace to the just and terror to the unjust.

❦

His appearance was like lightning, and his clothing white as snow.
For fear of him the guards shook and became like dead men.
But the angel said to the women, "Do not be afraid . . ."
Matthew 28:4-5

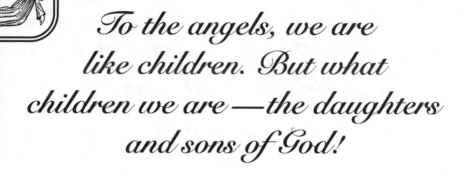

*To the angels, we are
like children. But what
children we are — the daughters
and sons of God!*

❧

My point is this: heirs, as long as they are minors, are no better
than slaves, though they are the owners of all the property; but they remain
under guardians and trustees until the date set by the father.
Galatians 4:1-2

In ancient times, some people believed the angels were gods. This did not please the angels themselves!

❧

Do not let anyone disqualify you, insisting on self-abasement and worship of angels, dwelling on visions, puffed up without cause by a human way of thinking, and not holding fast to the head, from whom the whole body, nourished and held together by its ligaments and sinews, grows with a growth that is from God.
Colossians 2:18-19

God has given us the abilities to discern truth and to think critically. Don't be afraid to use them.

❧

Beloved, do not believe every spirit, but test the spirits to see whether they are from God; for many false prophets have gone out into the world. By this you know the Spirit of God: every spirit that confesses that Jesus Christ has come in the flesh is from God, and every spirit that does not confess Jesus is not of God.
1 John 4:1-3

Angels are spirits, and the same Hebrew word that means "spirit" also means "wind" and "breath."

After this I saw four angels standing at the four corners of the earth,
holding back the four winds of the earth so that no wind
could blow on earth or sea or against any tree.
Revelation 7:1

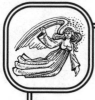

*The life of an angel is filled
with joy unspeakable
and full of glory.*

❧

*Happy are those who live in your house,
ever singing your praise.*
Psalms 84:4

EILEEN ELIAS FREEMAN directs the Angel Watch™ Network and publishes the *Angel Watch™ Journal*, a bimonthly magazine. She is the author of the bestselling book, *Touched by Angels*. Eileen holds a master's degree in theology from the University of Notre Dame and a B.A. in Comparative Religion from Barnard College.